ATTITUDE:
The **WINNER'S** Edge!

Also by Doris Gothard:

SEVEN STEPS TO WEALTH

Email us at Wealthsda@DorisGothard.com or

To order, visit us at www.dorisgothard.com

for information on other products.

The Power of a New Attitude

Attitude: The Winner's Edge

Email us at Attitude@DorisGothard.com or

To order, visit us at www.dorisgothard.com

for information on other products.

ATTITUDE: The WINNER'S Edge!
Copyright @ 2011 by Doris Gothard

Printed by Lightning Source, an INGRAM Content Company

Library of Congress Control Number: 2012903078
Gothard, Doris.
Title: ATTITUDE: The WINNER'S Edge

All rights reserved. No part of this publication may be reproduced or transmitted in any form or by any means, electronic or mechanical, including photocopying, recording, or by any information storage and retrieval system, without the prior written permission from the publisher or the author. Contact the publisher for information on foreign rights.

The author assumes full responsibility for the accuracy of all facts and quotations as cited in this book.

This book was

Edited by Sue Pauling

Illustration by Tara J. Hannon, Creative Designer
Meant for a Moment Designs
www.tarajhannon.com
www.meantforamoment.com

Interior Design by Carolyn Sheltraw
www.csheltraw.com
Typeset: Adobe InDesign CS5

Doris Gothard's Photo on Back Cover by
Photographer, Dr. Jeffery T. Baker, DDS SMILES by BAKER
www.smilesbybaker.com

Doris Gothard.—1st ed.
Attitude is not created by what happens to us but by our *attitude* toward each happening /
   1. Self-Improvement: Motivational & Inspirational. 2. Personal Growth – Self-Esteem. 3. Personal Growth – Success.

ISBN: 978-0-615-60520-3 (Case Laminate)
ISBN: 978-0-9860055-0-3 (Perfect Bound)

www.DorisGothard.com

Printed in the United States of America

ABOUT THE COVER

The first time I crossed the finish line after running a 50-yard dash on an outdoor running track for the first time, an eagerness for successful completion surged over me. Choosing to have a positive attitude is a celebration of change, crossing, determination, effort, and success. The illustrations on the book cover prove that anyone can do it!

— *Doris Gothard*

THE WINNER'S EDGE AMONG BIRDS

There is no spectacle in the whole world of birds so inspiring as the soaring eagle floating on outstretched wings.

Something of the grandeur of that spectacle is due to the association with the great part that the eagle has played in history and to the almost supernatural powers attributed to him in legend and myth. But it is not wholly this aura of tradition that invests the eagle, whenever seen, with an interest more compelling and more nearly universal than that inspired by any other feathered creature. He is in his own right a bird of unsurpassed power and majesty, the finest and strongest of the great order of martial birds, the Raptores of birds of prey, which include in their number the swiftest and most formidable of the denizens of the air.

The eagle is among birds what the lion is among beasts; and in many ways his appeal to the imagination is even stronger than that of the lion, due largely to his habit of soaring to magnificent heights, to his superb and commanding aspect when standing at rest, and to the spectacular and imposing nature of his aerial evolutions when seeking and pursuing his prey.

–Herbert Sass[1]

DEDICATED

This book is dedicated with the greatest love and affection to my family, friends and …

To God for giving me everything – life and the passion to do His work.

To my young friends,
who give encouragement.
– Abigail, Abrianna, Allonna, Amber Lyons, Angel, Anyae', Ashlon, Ava, Aydan, Cameron, Cariel, Carmiela, Carmiya, Chanell, Cheyenne, Christina, Courtney, Diamond, Donovan, Eva-Leigh, Eve, Geniah, Gervase II (Gerger), Iman, Issabella, Jada, Jaliya, Janai, Jordyn, Joy, Kaden, Kadence, Kahlia, Kayla, Kennedy, Khloe, Kyle, Layla, LeiLani, Lindsey, Madison, Marleigh, Messiah, Nicole, Paisley, Queen, Rylie Imani, Savanna, Savonne, Shawnica, Shidiamond, Telia-Denise, and Zarya –

To my teen and young adults,
who embrace change.
– Alana, Arianna, Ashlon, Ashlyn, Beautie, Briana, Danielle, Jessica, Kara, Keona, Kiy'Ana, Leigha, Lorelle, Marquitta, Morgan, Rhonda, Shelby, Verenisse, and Wanda –

To my role models,
who serve as an example.
– Adriana, Alexis, April, Ashlon, Audrey, Brandie, Christina, Christine, Cortney, Courtney, Crystal, Danielle, Dr. Jessica, Ellie, Francis, Gabi, Grace, Izairius, Jaliyah, Jameela, Jasmin, Juliane, Kanesha, Katherine, Kitty, Kreshona, Kristyn, Lauren Nicole, Linda, Maryam, Queanna, Sam, Sharell, Siera, Tiffany, Vernesher and Atty Carmen –

To the eagles, athletes and pathfinders,
who are honest, brave and passionate team players.
– Brian, Caleb Darensbourg, Camerin, Carl, Charles, Christopher, Clayton, CoryJr, Demetrius, Dennis, Devin Gabriel, DJ, Domonic, Jeremiah, Donovan, Donovan Rasheed Malachi, EugeneJr, Felix, Franqui II, Gavin, GlyneG III, Isaiah, Jaelen, James II, Jayden, Jaylin, Jeramiah, Jevontae', Jonathan, Jordan, Joshua, Josiah, Kaden, Kai, KJ, Kyle, LeonJr, Matthew, Michael, Myles, Reece, Ricky II, Robert, Ryan, Sam, Sameer, SamJr, Samuel III, Samuel Kelly, Semajay, Steven, Teron, Terrance Jalen (TJ), Tristan, Tristan II, Tyler, Xavier, Zachary and CharlesO IV –

My executive leaders-in-training.

To the Cast of
"I BELIEVE"

TABLE OF CONTENTS

Introduction 1
    Inside Story: The Journey Begins 5

The Power to Choose 7
    Inside Story: The Power of Two Words 15

Good Attitudes = Good Behaviors 21
    Inside Story: The Attitude Test 43

Attitude is Your Responsibility. 49
    Inside Story: My Aunt 83

Make Right Choices 85
    Inside Story: Attitude Story 103

A Mistake Is Not a Failure 106
    Inside Story: Attitude Math 121

The Attitude Golden Rule 123
    Inside Story: An Inspirational Memoir 131

The Stages of Your Life 137

A Final Glimpse of Our Attitude. 141

End Notes 151

A GIVING ATTITUDE IS THE SECRET TO ★ SUCCESS ★

INTRODUCTION

Attitude is a reflection of the person inside. Attitude is the *key* to a better life. When you feel good about *yourself,* others feel good about *you!*

Everything we do in life must be done with and through other people. What affects them most is our attitude, something that can be controlled. Most people wake up each morning without thinking about their attitudes. They wake up expecting the worst. Every day they wake up expecting things will just be terrible, and they are! They react to whatever happens to them. They have a defeatist attitude.

Success means having a good attitude. Success means having skills, such as the ability to read and write. If you can read, you can do anything. Success means having work experience, good appearance, skills, and yes – good grades. But, the ultimate success in life is having a positive *attitude*. Most people are not successful in life because they are defeated by the *hard facts* about their failures. It's not the *hard facts* that defeat a person; it's a person's *attitude toward* those facts. Failure is only possible for the one who believes he will *fail!* Learn from both your successes and mistakes in a positive and constructive way.

There are people in the world today who believe they have *no* future. They feel hopeless! Making choices is very difficult for them because they feel anger toward their parents, teachers, or friends. They sometimes have feelings of guilt, lack of confidence, low self-esteem, or they are not competitive enough, have ineffective communication skills (both oral and written), or are not goal setters.

Attitude: The Winner's Edge is about being a player on the NBA team called **N**othing **B**eats **A**ttitude – the winner's edge to a better life. You will learn that "your head is your greatest asset and that you must keep it under control at all times." In just one moment, you can make a decision that will shape the rest of your life. At the moment of choice – choose the right behavior! Choose the right attitude!

Attitude:

- ✔ Expect the best and get it!
- ✔ Expect to reach the goals YOU set for YOURSELF!
    - There is no good reason why YOU can't be as successful as anyone else!
    - Most people are generally no smarter than YOU!
- ✔ Expect to succeed more often than fail!
- ✔ Expect the best and get it!

Nothing **B**eats **A**ttitude (NBA)! Be a player on our NBA team. At the moment of choice, believe in yourself. Do what is right. Avoid what is wrong. Do the best you can. Be the best you can be.

Attitude counts! It is the *winner's edge!* When looking for a job, remember that most employers aren't looking for experience only. Employers look more for **attitude**, enthusiasm, personality, and a good track record of achievements rather than hands-on experience. Lack of experience is the last reason you aren't offered a job opportunity. The most common reasons job seekers are not offered the job are

- Poor attitude
- Lack of self-confidence

- Inability to speak or express yourself
- Lack of preparation
- Poor appearance
- Etc.

Attitude counts! It is the **winner's edge!** Our attitudes say to the world what we expect in return. We should always radiate the attitude of well-being and confidence.

A positive attitude is everything when it may seem that we are at a low point in life. Our thoughts tend to react to our thinking, and negative thinking generates negative thoughts. Negative thoughts generate more negative thoughts, and negative people will eventually begin to rub off on you!

Learn to associate with positive people. Positive thinking people generate positive OPTIMISTIC thoughts that affect the world around us – positively! Would others say you have a positive attitude or a negative attitude? Would others describe you as a very creative person? Would others say your disposition is one of patience and sensitivity toward other people? Would others say you were enthusiastic about your work and about life? Are you confident that you always do the best that you can with what you know and view all life's experiences as opportunities for personal growth? Are you gaining new understanding every day, which allows you to learn from both your successes and mistakes in a positive and constructive way?

I believe that our attitudes are like windows, taking in light. If our light is filled with the darkness of negative attitudes – the whole body is affected. There is nothing like knowing who you are, where you are, and where you're going. **Attitude Is – The Winner's Edge!** Expect the best, and you will get it!

Doris

Doris (right) picking cotton with her sister Roxie (left) in the Alabama Cotton Fields • illustrated by Tara Harmon.

INSIDE STORY

THE JOURNEY BEGINS
By Doris Gothard

As a child growing-up in the Alabama cotton fields, nothing came easy for me. Nurtured by my grandparents (Anthony and Bessie), mother and step-father (Geneva and Pop) aunts and uncles (Sooten and G, Aleain and JB, Mollie and William, Mamie T and Wash, Uncle Ted, Nancy and Gene) – I received an abundance of love from my family. They talked to me about the importance of having a positive attitude in every circumstance. In my journey to a new attitude, I started working in the cotton fields of Alabama as soon as I was able to walk. It's true! I picked and picked and picked cotton. It was so hot, I would pray for rain so my work day could end. It was an all day, sun up to sunset job.

From childhood, I learned to have a positive attitude and good work ethic, no matter what the circumstance. I worked as a hired day worker, picking cotton and cleaning homes as a maid until I enrolled as a freshman in college. The cotton fields of Alabama sparked the beginning of my attitude journey to unlock my potential! Changing my attitude about my circumstances in life has been an awesome responsibility!

Picking cotton and cleaning homes made me a very hard-working individual. I was able to finish college and have a very successful career.

Recently, on a hot Alabama summer day, I was reunited after more than 50 years with the family that I picked cotton for; my first employer – the Cobb Family. They said they were proud of me and my success in life and always knew I would be successful. The Cobb's are my family. Our reunion and my work in the Alabama cotton fields will be remembered with *gratitude*.

The Power to Choose

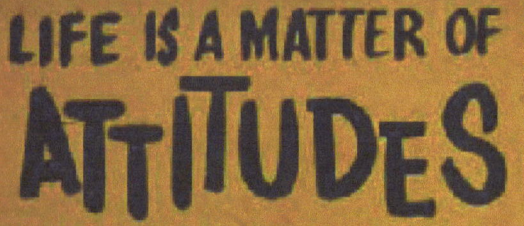
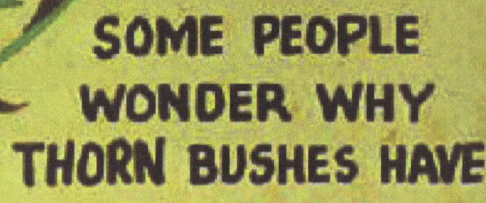

Good attitudes are demonstrated by being positive, encouraging, cooperative, etc. No one knows your thoughts, but most people can identify a person who has a good attitude. Here are some statements about someone having a good attitude: "He or she is friendly and has a good attitude" or "He or she has a positive attitude."

You are the only one who has the "power to choose" your attitude.

Virtually everyone remembers that one special person who earned the title of mentor or coach because of the help he/she gave you. Maybe it was a teacher, parent, grandparent, uncle, sister, or a neighbor. Maybe it was someone who appreciated your potential, gave you candid feedback, or forced you to be honest with yourself—someone who kept you on track and inspired you to go further than you ever thought possible.

Before you can achieve the type of life you DESIRE,

You must become the type of INDIVIDUAL you DESIRE to be.

My nephew Gervase is the mentor for his younger brother Marcus.

My nephew Marcus is now the mentor for his nephew Terrance Jalen (TJ), Gervase's oldest son.

Choose a mentor or coach to help you achieve your goals in life.

Join the Attitude NBA Team: **N**othing **B**eats **A**ttitude! Know who

YOU are and what YOU want in life, and good things will start

happening for you, too.

A young man named Joe chose his Uncle Don (my husband) to be his mentor and coach. Joe is a high school principal, recently promoted to Assistant School Superintendent in Madison, Wisconsin. Joe is currently a Ph.D. student at a university in Madison, Wisconsin.

Gabi (14), Grace (11), Gavin (8), wife Mary, and our nephew Joe.

THE POWER OF TWO WORDS

By Joe Gothard

May 5, 2011

Thank you, Uncle Don! I appreciate your steady presence and guidance in my life. I am convinced that the message of education you imprinted in our conversations over the years has been an extrinsic factor in my development. Yesterday was very intense. I had to bring a staff together who four years ago thought they would have to call in the National Guard because the school was broken and hurting. Recently, my days have been spent as a reflective and authentic instructional leader. I am spending more time on school-wide literacy and very little on eradicating gang banging in school. I have an awesome team, and we have systems in place that have gained us regional attention with community and school folks from all over visiting and writing us about how we have suppressed gang involvement in our school. I say all of this because I am ready for my next challenge. You see, people don't realize this, but other than saying something about my mother, I had better not ever hear you say, "These kids can't read or write." Those are fighting words!

It has taken me many years to realize my academic potential, and much of my inadequate feelings were influenced by the relationships and expectations of the adults around me. In my new position I will have the opportunity to ensure that all of our graduates are equipped with speaking, listening, reading, writing and reasoning skills...all kids.

So, enough of my manifesto. Our daughter Gabi is playing in a volleyball tournament in Grand Rapids this weekend. We are leaving around noon tomorrow (this is only my second tournament, so your advice was spot on). Hopefully the weather cooperates because we are going to stop at Notre Dame. I want my kids to walk one of the most beautiful and historic universities in the world. They also know that I am proud of you and your accomplishments as a student and alumnus.

Have a great day, and my best to Doris.

    Love,
    Joe

THE GOTHARD FAMILY

Gabi (14), Gavin (8), wife Mary,
our nephew Joe and Grace (11).

Joe learned to think, act, talk, walk, and conduct himself as would the person he wished to become. What makes Joe's story so important? Joe is our nephew, and we are so proud of him. Joe learned from his uncle Don that hard work, preparation, and a good attitude are the keys to success.

If you believe you will succeed, you will succeed. Try to avoid focusing on your failures. Always expect to succeed more often than fail. Think positively. Expect to reach your goals. Choose a mentor or a coach to help you achieve your goals. Expect the best, and you'll get it! **NBA** - **N**othing **B**eats **A**ttitude!

You, and only you, are in charge of your attitude! A great attitude will propel you forward. There is very little difference in most people, but that little difference makes a BIG difference. The LITTLE difference is *attitude*. The BIG difference is whether you have a *good* attitude or a *bad* attitude. Choose to have a good attitude by being positive, encouraging, loving, humble, teachable, cooperative, considerate, selfless, loyal, and persevering.

Roger Van Oech in his book *A Whack on the Side of the Head*[5] wrote that people have certain attitudes that "lock" their thinking into the status quo and keep them asking for more of the same. He called them "mental locks." You can break the habit by preparing yourself to make good, educated decisions. The key to unlocking mental locks is to choose the right attitude.

Nothing **B**eats **A**chievement!

As a teenager, our son LeWayne (see picture below), had mental locks during his teenage and young adult years. He made all the wrong choices as a teenager and young adult. But, the "sleeping giant" woke-up and unlocked the mental locks.

He changed his attitude and unlocked his potential. LeWayne made a decision to go back to school and finish his college education. We are proud of our son LeWayne, who graduated with a Bachelor's Degree and a Master's Degree in Business Administration (MBA), with honors. His goal is to enroll in a university doctoral program and receive his PhD. LeWayne is an example of a young man who changed his bad behaviors to good and achieved good results.

Our son LeWayne, proud MBA graduate, *with distinction.*

Our only grandson Justin, an automotive design college student.

YOU SHAPE YOUR LIFE BY YOUR ATTITUDE

It is how you think or act towards a person or thing.

UNIVERSAL LAW: One translates into reality the thoughts and attitudes one holds in one's mind.

GOOD attitudes = **GOOD RESULTS**

BAD attitudes and you're licked before you start.

Good Attitudes

=

Good Behaviors

Good attitudes = Good Behaviors! However, the equation most people use to identify **bad attitudes** in people is: **"Bad Attitudes = Bad Behaviors."** When you exhibit negative outward displays of bad behavior such as, "I can cheat on this test" or "I can spend all this money on myself"—these are examples of bad attitudes and bad behaviors to avoid—cheating and selfishness. Don't mimic the bad attitudes and bad behaviors of others.

Good Attitudes and Good Behaviors = Good Results.

There is a lasting and powerful influence our behaviors have on our attitudes. Use your attitude to influence good behavior. Spend time with people such as teachers, coaches, parents, grandparents, uncles, sisters, friends, or neighbors who encourage and help you stay on track.

It is amazing how our attitude influences our behavior. Our attitude makes a powerful effect on our relationships with other people by our responses, actions, reactions, conduct, and deportment. From the time we are born, our attitude has the power to either bring us closer to others or push them away from us. When we change our attitude, we change our behavior and our relationships with others.

Remember the Equation:
Bad Attitudes = Bad Behaviors.
Good Attitudes = Good Behaviors.

When it comes to attitude, a picture is worth a thousand words. How people perceive you visually is more powerful than what people hear you say verbally. Everyone is responsible for his/her own actions. There is power in attitude—both oral and visual.

Your attitude can be used to improve the attitudes of other people. There are ways you should change your attitude to do things differently. You can make a BIG difference in someone else's life when you change your old attitude to a *new attitude*. When you change your attitude, you change your world. *That's power*!

Attitude shows a lot in how we dress. The clothes you wear say a lot about your attitude. If you want to achieve success in life, your attitude about dress is very important! Your dress is how you perceive success and failure that makes the difference in your attitude. When you have an attitude of self-confidence and self-respect, it will affect what others think about you. Here are ten decisions people make about YOU—from YOUR dress. They form an opinion about your …

1. Environment
2. Education
3. Trustworthiness or Untrustworthiness
4. Job Title
5. Prestige
6. Status
7. Culture
8. Integrity
9. Attitude
10. Success

Your attitude is either your best friend or your worst enemy, your greatest asset or your greatest liability. If someone says,

- "He has a poor attitude."
- "She is dressed inappropriately."
- "He has to change his attitude or else."
- "Her attitude is positive."
- "Her negative attitude towards her work assignment makes her uncooperative."
- "They do as they like because of their attitude."
- "They don't associate with those people because of their attitude toward them as a group."

When these things are said about you …..

Have you ever had someone coerce you to DO something you did not want to do that lead to such things as drinking alcohol, using drugs, or getting in trouble with the law and your parents? PEERS who encourage you to do such things are persons, encouraging, errors, rudeness and stupidity, an expression attributed to Dr. Ben Carson. If the answer to the question is yes, here is "Your Attitude is Showing Equation":

Bad Attitudes = Bad Behaviors.

Have you ever had someone convince you NOT to do something you were planning to do, and it turned out well? If the answer is yes, here is "Your Attitude is Showing Equation":

Good Attitudes = Good Behaviors.

The good attitude equation can benefit you by helping you learn something, avoid breaking the law or getting into trouble with your parents, have a new experience, overcome fear, and find new friendships, encouragement and good advice. It also helps define who you are and how you feel about things going on in your life.

My nephew Marcus has a good attitude. He made good choices. He finished high school with honors, received the Governor's Academic Scholarship Award, went to college, and graduated from a university in Georgia. Today, Marcus is a Technical Support Specialist in Atlanta, Georgia, employed by the largest technology services provider in the world. He found his best friend and asked her to marry him.

Right Attitude and Right Choices = Good Results.

My nephew Marcus and his beautiful wife Mayelyn.

Everyone is influenced by other people, including PEERS who don't exhibit the right attitude or make right choices. Every day someone will influence your attitude in a manner similar or acceptable to themselves. The influence of any PEER group can affect the attitude of any individual. The influence can be negative or positive.

Remember, perception is everything! People tend to reflect back to you – the attitude they see in you. Whether you're in elementary school, high school, college or already working as an adult, proper dress paves the way for a clear path in leadership. Any display in our dress perceived as disrespectful is RUDE. You wouldn't want to miss out on a job opportunity or not be selected for a training program that would help you become an officer in the world's strongest fighting force just because someone perceived your attire to be inappropriate.

PEERS

PERSONS
ENCOURAGING
ERRORS
RUDENESS
STUPIDITY

ATTITUDE: The WINNER'S Edge! • 29

PERSONS

Make a decision not to allow anyone to cause you to react in any situation. Some bad attitudes may be influenced by PERSONS who encourage you to display a bad attitude. Some bad attitude examples are as follows: "He was showing some attitude during class today, so the teacher sent him to the office" "You need to change your bad attitude" "I don't know what the problem is, but she has a real attitude."

The key to dealing with a bad attitude is self-confidence. Avoid unpleasant outcomes at all costs. Learn to be yourself and make your own decisions, regardless of what others think. Listen to your gut. Hang with people who feel the same way you do. If a situation feels dangerous, learn to feel comfortable saying "no." The most important decision is how you chose to react. Learn to make good choices. Your attitude may seem trivial now, but it will be the key to your success later on. Make sure your friends are not always encouraging you to display distracting behaviors.

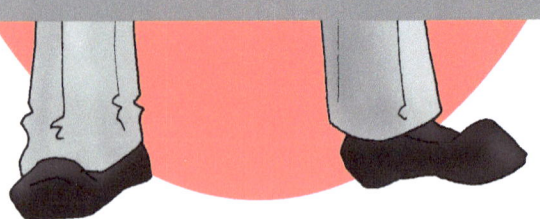

Something done wrong and left wrong is an ERROR – in need of correction. ERRORS can a misspelled word, inappropriate choices in peers, or bad behaviors. You are the only person who has the power to avoid mistakes when choosing your peers, bad behavior or other inappropriate choices. Avoid **errors** in your choices and associations with others.

To show people who YOU are – YOU don't have to do it in a negative way. Be positive! Learn to be respectful in your attitude towards other people and in your dress. Always dress for success. Dress appropriately for every occasion.

If you are dressing for a job interview, follow these simple guidelines:

- Women should wear a simple hair style, suit or dress or matching jacket, neutral-colored sheer hose, simple pumps, and a minimum of makeup; this is typical attire required for a job interview, meeting or workplace.
- Men should wear a conservative suit or slacks and jacket, white shirt, contrasting tie, shined shoes, matching belt and over-the calf socks. This is typical attire required for a job interview, meeting or workplace.

Always inquire about the proper dress code for each occasion. Rudeness in ones dress is inherently disruptive.

Mistakes will happen. Most mistakes can be corrected. Learn to associate with people who have the same high standard as you do. Learn to develop friendships with people who will help keep you on the right course. Look on the brighter side. When you get home, a special treat awaits – as well as the most cherished reward of a mentor's hard-earned approval that you made the decision to change your attitude and change your future.

That's a winner's edge!

Here is a picture of two of tomorrow's leaders (my nieces) who are straight "A" students - Jaliyah (14)(left) who loves band and choir and Ashlon (16) (right) who loves ROTC.

Physical activity is the *winner's edge.* Organized outdoor activities train leaders to lead. Some school programs offer tuition assistance by granting numerous scholarships to members who qualify. Youth oriented school programs provide education and leadership development training to high school students through programs that inspire youth to be problem solvers, decision makers, and future leaders in their communities. Consider connecting with a group of instrumental musicians in an outdoor school marching band or join a program to develop the next generation of technology and leadership. That's the *winner's edge!*

BELIEVE TO WIN!

**BELIEVING MAY NOT WIN EVERYTHING......
BUT WITHOUT BELIEF YOU WIN VERY LITTLE**

INSIDE STORY

THE ATTITUDE TEST

Here is a story about a father and his two sons[6]. The wise father wanted to teach his sons a valuable lesson about life. One morning he took them on a long hike around the lake near their home. Before they left the house, the father instructed the boys to bring their backpacks.

"I am conducting an experiment, boys," said the father. "So don't ask any questions until we get home, and I will explain." The boys agreed.

From time as they walked along the country road, the father would bend down pick up a rock and place it in one of their backpacks. At another point, the father would stop for a moment take a rock or two from out of one or both boys' backpacks. This same scenario continued throughout the day. Finally, just before sunset, the boys and their father returned home. When they reached the house, the two boys were tired. Their backpacks were heavy with a variety of rocks, and they were thankful that they didn't have to carry them on their backs anymore.

Now, warm and comfortable, sitting on their family-room couch, one boy asked, "Dad, can you tell us now about your experiment?"

The boys were curious, probing, "Why did you keep putting rocks in our backpacks and then take some out?"

The father explained that when he was young, his dad conducted this experiment with him, and he has always remembered its important lesson. "Today," the father explained, "I gave you both an attitude test."

The boys questioned, "What? What's an attitude test?"

The father replied, "As we were hiking, I was listening carefully to everything you two boys said, and whenever one of you complained or spoke negatively about a person or a situation, I picked up a rock and put it in your backpack."

The boys stared at each other wide-eyed, with a confused look on their faces. Continuing, the father said, "But, when either of you displayed a grateful, generous attitude, when you spoke of the best in others or a belief in yourself, I removed a rock from the bag."

After 60 seconds of complete silence, the father asked his sons to take a look at the backpacks they had been carrying all day. "Wrong thinking, regrets, frustrations, and unforgiveness are like those rocks. You can hold them in your mind, just like you carried them in your backpack," the father said. "If your mind becomes too cluttered with discouragement, it can prevent great things from happening in your future." The father hugged his boys and concluded, "Always remember the power of a positive attitude. Pay attention to your thoughts. Listen to the words you use, and notice how you say them."

SELF-TALK

- I'm going to change, learn, and improve from this.
- I'm really excited about this opportunity.
- I'm proud to see new developments in my growth.
- Every contact with another person is a learning experience.
- I feel a greater depth in myself today.
- The future holds GREAT THINGS in store for me!
- I am creative and innovative.

SELF-TALK

We must choose wisely, not permitting destructive, toxic thoughts to rule our minds. Attitude is everything. When attitudes go down, our potential goes down with it. When attitudes go up, our potential goes up too.

Choose your attitude. Wake up every morning expecting the best out of your day, and you will get it. Dream big! Rise above challenges with a positive attitude. Claim the right to choose a positive attitude every day and unlock your potential to live a victorious and successful life. Wake up each morning and do some attitude: **SELF-TALK!**

Your **ATTITUDE** is the one thing you have totally under your control.

You may not be able to:
- control inflation, but how you <u>view</u> it is up to you.
- avoid having a flat tire, but how you <u>think</u> about it is your choice.

ALL YOUR LIFE YOU WILL HAVE PROBLEMS, BUT EVERY PROBLEM HAS A…….

SOLUTION

Attitude Is Your Responsibility

Learn a new skill.

Choose a role model.

Learn a new skill. There are individuals willing to use their skills to help affect positive changes in others. They help make us better people by sharing their expertise. It is true that not everything is fair in the real world and not all environments are accepting of differences in people. But, life is not always about race, color, hair, or sex. When some people achieve more than others, it's more about having a good attitude than one's abilities that determines one's success in life. Learn a new skill. Choose a role model.

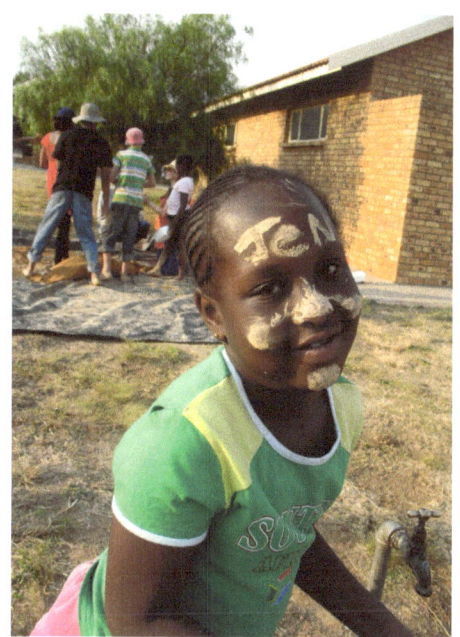
Hello! My Name is Jen.

Hello! My Name is Maryam.

Know who you are and be proud, just like Jen and Maryam (my great niece). Nothing is always fair in the real world. Not all environments are accepting of differences in people. Life is not always about race, color, hair or sex. When some people achieve more than others, it's more about having a good attitude than one's abilities that determines success in life. Choose a role model. Learn a new skill.

Look in the mirror! It's time to take charge! Your attitude is a reflection of the person inside. You have the power to choose your attitude. Keep your mind on things that are good. If you dwell on negative things, your attitude will reflect negative things, and you will be whipped before you start your day. Look in the mirror. Part of the right attitude is to have a *"winning attitude."*

It doesn't matter what we do
until we accept ourselves.
Once we accept ourselves,
it doesn't matter what we do.

Accept yourself! Choose to have a positive attitude

no matter what you decide to do in life.

"Tomorrow, you promise yourself, will be different, yet,

tomorrow is too often a repetition of today."[7]

– James T. McCay

I choose my attitude in every circumstance

Our attitude, opinions, and thoughts do matter! Only our own thoughts, words, and attitudes can hurt us. The path to a successful attitude is NOT as difficult as we might think. Each time we overcome an obstacle, our path to success becomes easier. Our attitude will, to a large degree, determine the eventual results in our life.

Say out **LOUD** to yourself ….My *new attitude* is one of life's privileges. MY success in life will come as a result of MY being prepared. MY success in life will not be a matter of luck but hard work, preparation, and a positive attitude. It will take hard work to be successful. But—MY rewards in life will be the results of MY efforts. The way I talk about MYSELF today, creates MY tomorrow. MY good attitude is a continuous journey. MY good attitude will help me through tough times.

We can be shaped & molded by our problems,
or we can be challenged & motivated by them.
To welcome a problem without resentment is
to cut its size in half.
We can see our setbacks as adversities or . . .
as adventures, confinements or challenges,
dungeons or doorways.
  "A" is the author of many songs;
 tribulation is inspiration for many poems.
  "A" causes some people to break,
    others to break records.

Your attitude will shape your life. In every circumstance, choose to have a positive attitude. A poor attitude will make others miserable, including you. We are either the masters or the victims of our attitudes. It's a matter of personal choice—blessing or curse. Make the right choice! A positive attitude will take you places you always dreamed of.

GET OUT OF YOUR OWN WAY!

Little things like weather conditions, technology, personal situations, environment, and other people can undermine your choice of attitude. The news, waiting (in traffic, at the doctor's office, the postal service, the grocery store), or airline delays can undermine your attitude. Things that break—the car won't start, the VCR won't play, the cable television network is down—can undermine your attitude. Generation differences and problems with relatives or neighbors (the way they act, the way they look) can undermine your attitude. Having to work or losing something of value to you can affect your attitude.

Are you killing yourself with your own attitude? Choose to have a positive attitude every day. The problem is not the <u>problem</u>. The problem is your ATTITUDE about the problem. Choose a positive attitude for every circumstance.

Treat every contact with another person as a learning experience. There are indelible links between the CHOICES we make and what we accomplish. Get excited about the opportunity to choose. The future holds great things in store for you when you make right choices in life. Make a decision to change, learn, and improve the choices you make in life. Remember: You can choose your attitude.

When someone does something kind for you, recognize it. **Say, "Thank you."** Make others feel needed, important, and appreciated, and they will return the same to you. A simple "thank you" goes a long way.

Everyone likes to feel that they are of value and that they count. Encouraging words are essential to life. Just as a plant needs water, we all need a little encouragement from time to time. We all make mistakes. We all need encouragement from a helping hand to help us evaluate our mistakes. An attitude of gratitude is important because attitude truly is everything! It drives virtually every decision you make and how you live each day of your life. Attitude either propels you forward or holds you back. While the external circumstances in your life can be chaotic, your attitude is the key to a better life. Are you in need of encouragement? You are not alone. Be confident. Know what you want in life.

Eli Whitney had an OPTIMISTIC attitude. Eli Whitney's invention of the cotton gin revolutionized the cotton industry in the United States. Prior to his invention, farming cotton required hundreds of man-hours to separate the cottonseed from the raw cotton fibers. Many people said his machine would put thousands of people out of work. Instead, the invention made the production of cloth much cheaper, and millions of people were able to buy more clothing, which created countless jobs.

Charles Babbage had an OPTIMISTIC attitude. Charles Babbage invented the computer. When the computer was invented, many people believed they would lose their jobs. Almost everyone will agree that computers have improved how we communicate. Part of the right attitude is to look for the good in people and be open to the ideas of others. You too can dream the impossible! You can start your own business or become an inventor.

Maggie Lee Sayre had an OPTIMISTIC attitude. Maggie Lee Sayre was born deaf near Paducah, Kentucky, in 1920. She lived 51 years of her life on a river houseboat as her family made a living fishing throughout Kentucky and Tennessee. During her life she did not see her deafness as a handicap but an opportunity to unlock her potential. She used her camera to take black and white pictures that changed the way we view our world.

Madam C.J. Walker had an OPTIMISTIC attitude. Madam Walker, the first female millionaire, was born to slave parents who were sharecroppers in Delta, Louisiana. Her journey began in the cotton fields of the South. The people she worked for promoted her from the cotton fields to work as a washerwoman, and from washerwoman she was promoted to kitchen cook. Later in life she bought her own land, built her own factory, and promoted herself into the business of manufacturing hair products.

Harriet Tubman had an OPTIMISTIC attitude. Born in Maryland into slavery as a child, she was one of 11 children. She was beaten by the master she was hired to work for. At an early age she suffered a head wound when hit by a heavy metal weight which caused disabling health problems throughout her life. As a runaway slave, she fled for her life to Philadelphia to escape slavery in Maryland. Not satisfied with her own freedom, she returned immediately to Maryland to deliver hundreds of other slaves to freedom with the help of a network of activists and safe houses known as the Underground Railroad.

In spite of her numerous health challenges (severe headaches, dizziness, dreams, etc.), Harriet Tubman (known also as "Moses"), was a courageous fighter for women's suffrage and Civil Rights. In poor health, it was no easy task for her to mobilize slaves to freedom but with a positive attitude and determination, she was prepared to lead her people out of slavery.

Choose to have an OPTIMISTIC attitude. It will pave the way for you to unlock your potential! Change your attitude! Change your world!

Anything can be accomplished with the right attitude. Pump up your *new attitude* like you would pump up your "Sooper Pump, stylish, leather soft, supportive, and comfortable" tennis shoe.

Be curious to learn more. Curiosity in new ideas is an important trait of genius. Albert Einstein never stopped asking questions. He was curious. Curiosity builds on the best in new ideas. Curiosity is an attitude which expands the boundaries of our thinking. It says, "I know my assumptions about the world are incomplete, but I want to know more." Nothing beats a good attitude. Expand the boundaries of your thinking. Set high standards for yourself. Anything can be accomplished if you have a positive attitude.

Doris's friends – sisters Telia-Denise (9) and Eva-Leigh (11) (left) and Verenisse (15) (right).

If you believe you are going to succeed at piano, you will succeed! Believe in yourself, and you will succeed!

Perception is everything! Learn to see things in a new and different way. Your idea is just as good as someone else's idea. Most people are generally no smarter than you! There is no good reason why you can't be as successful as anyone else. Embrace your ideas. Be creative – embrace the spark to imagine and the daring to innovate. Discipline yourself to plan. Acquire the skills to do. Have the will to achieve.

You will KNOW you have the right attitude about new ideas when you can say, "I know my assumptions are incomplete, but I want to know more." Look for GOOD ideas everywhere.

Learn values that will help you build a positive "can-do" attitude such as humility, curiosity, empathy, and trust. Nothing beats a failure but a try. The most powerful force is what you say to yourself. Only our own thoughts, words, and attitudes can hurt us. Our attitude, opinions, and thoughts do matter. Never, ever feel like a failure. New opportunities lead to a new attitude. Never give up!

When faced with a challenge in life, try to discipline yourself to think positively. Positive things happen to positive people. When your attitude is positive, you will master your difficulties. Remember: Choose your *attitude*—Choose your *power!* DON'T let life's challenges get you down!

Jockey Eddie Arcaro lost his first 45 races. Michael Jordan was cut from his high school basketball team. You will not be remembered for the number of times you failed in the beginning, but for the number of times you succeeded in the end.

When you find yourself in a difficult situation, DON'T despair. Your head is your greatest asset. The chief purpose of your body is to carry your brain around. It is your mind, working in a calm, cool fashion that solves your problems. Failure is not the last word! Keep your thoughts under disciplined control—no drugs, no alcohol, no tobacco. Cultivate the right attitude that will help you succeed in the end.

Choose to see your setbacks as doorways to opportunities and adventures instead of adversities, confinements, challenges, and dungeons. When you welcome your problem without resentment, you can cut its size in half. You can be shaped and molded by your problems, or you can be challenged and motivated by them.

When we STAMP our own VALUE upon ourselves,

we cannot expect to pass for MORE or less.

The **right attitude** at the beginning of your journey to a new attitude in life will affect the outcome more than anything else. Say: **"Yes, I can! Yes, I will change my attitude!"** Since your mind can only hold one thought at a time, you should fill your mind with positive thoughts. Be willing to learn new things from others. Get really good at what you do. You are IN CHARGE. What you say, think, and do **builds confidence**! Build your confidence with a *new positive attitude.*

Walk like you matter! Radiate confidence. It is good when friends check out your *new attitude*. Now that's *power!* A negative attitude will never defeat a person with a positive attitude.

LEARN SOMETHING NEW

Make a decision to wake up every day with an attitude that says, "I am somebody. I am of value and worth, and I am going to learn something new today and live my life fully and joyfully."

Your attitude, more than anything else, will determine your success or failure. It is your **attitude** that will determine your **altitude** in life. For the rest of your life, expect the best and get it! Man is the only known creature who can reshape and remold himself by altering his attitude. Your attitude is important.

Very little is needed to make for a happy life when you have good health, family, friends, and a positive attitude. Feed your attitude daily. Learn to develop a good attitude by dwelling on things that are good. When we dwell on negative thoughts, our attitude will reflect negative thoughts. Our attitudes are intertwined with the roles we try to play in life…how we see ourselves, how we really are, and how others see us.

Make prayer and meditation a part of your life.

A life without prayer is like a computer without the software. Life without prayer is life without HOPE. Life without prayer is boring and empty. Prayer is like a passion for something to come true that seems impossible to do. PRAYER is a good thing. It is the force that energizes our faith every day!

The greatest privilege God gives to us is the freedom to approach Him at any time. Trouble and perplexity drive us to prayer, and prayer drives away trouble and perplexity. Nothing can tilt things more dramatically in our favor than prayer! Prayer changes things! When we depend upon man, we get what man can do; when we depend upon prayer, we get what God can do.

My nephew Gervase with his wife Joanil and their sons Gervase II (Gerger on left) and Donovan.

INSIDE STORY

MY AUNT
By Gervase Draper

12-year-old Gervase chose his Aunt Doris to be his mentor. Gervase is now a college graduate with a wife, two boys, and another child on the way. Gervase is currently an IT Voice Analyst working for a large telephony services company in Atlanta, Georgia. Since his childhood, Gervase has always admired his Aunt Doris.

When his 7th grade teacher asked him to write a paper about a person he most admired, here is what Gervase wrote about his Aunt Doris:

MY AUNT

I have a beautiful aunt both in spirit and in body who has smooth yellow skin accented by hazel green eyes that gleam like the stars of heaven. Her elegant clothing is always right for the occasion. She smiles a lot, so you can see the beauty of her happiness deep within her eyes. Her walk is a stride that says at all times "I Am Somebody."

What makes Gervase's Story so important? Gervase learned that the key to success is a good attitude. Gervase is our nephew, and we are so proud of him.

TODAY, OUR WORLD EXISTS BECAUSE OF

TOMORROW WILL GROW FROM

CHOICES

WE MADE YESTERDAY

YOU AND I MAKE TODAY!

Make Right Choices

Family is *the winner's edge* to developing a good attitude and helping to make right choices. The Lyons family believes in early involvement to help their sons Jordan (14) and Camerin (10) learn to think about the importance of attitude, education, and making good decisions in life – including sports. Elliott and Kelly support their sons in basketball and football by their presence at games. Elliot says: "Kelly and I are truly blessed with two awesome boys, and we love them dearly. It is my pleasure and honor to be their father as they continue to grow and develop into young men." Learn to make right choices with family involvement. It's the *winner's edge!*

Left to Right: Elmer and LaVella (Grandparents), Kelly (Mother), Camerin, Jordan, and Elliott (Father).

Jordan (14)

Quarterback Jordan, leading the team after a tough game.

Camerin (10)

Camerin pushing the ball. That's the winner's edge!

Jordan and Camerin show that attitude makes a difference.

Don't waste your time discussing personal problems

There is power in our CHOICES. They can be good as well as bad. Remember to make CHOICES that encourage positive attitudes. Your CHOICE is the **Attitude Winner's Edge**.

Our friends are important in our lives, but try not to waste too much time sharing too much personal information with friends who can't solve your problem. What affects them the most is our attitude. Avoid talking about serious personal problems with anyone who can't solve your problem.

Use the power of your CHOICE to choose your friends very carefully. Choose people you can learn more from and who can be positive role models. Learn to demonstrate positive attitudes and a manner of conducting yourself positively at all times. Learn to develop positive relationships with people who yearn to learn. Learn to make your own decision, regardless of what another person is encouraging you to do. Listen to your gut. Feel comfortable saying "no."

WE TEND TO ACCEPT IDEAS THAT REINFORCE OUR ATTITUDES!

- PEOPLE AND THINGS +
- WAY OF LIVING +
- MONEY & VALUE +
- JOB & WORK +
- GOALS & AMBITIONS +
- RELIGION & CHARITY +
- RIGHT & WRONG +
- POLITICS +

There is an old saying "a friend sticketh closer than a brother." Our choice of friends (based on societal groups, age, grade, status, etc.) are a part of our daily lives. Our friends are persons among our age group with whom we associate. A true friend is a person, regardless of his/her age, whom you can trust.

The question is this: "Do you know the difference between your friends and your *true friends* when it comes to *trust?* And does it really matter? Yes. It really does matter! There is a difference, and there are times when you need to know that difference. Knowing the difference between peers and having a true friend whom you can trust is: **The Winner's Edge!**

Choose friends who encourage you to be creative and innovative. Develop positive relationships with friends who feel the same way you do. In other words, hang with those who have the same positive attitude. There is power in choosing friends who encourage you not to exhibit bad attitudes. What affects other people the most is your attitude. Choose friends who display positive attitudes towards others.

By the same token, learn how to respond to negative peer pressure by being self-confident. Don't hesitate or be afraid to ask for an adult's help in any situation that makes you feel uncomfortable.

As you *begin* your day, make a decision to be POSITIVE

Doris's friend Jasmin is a mentor to her friend Lei Lani.

Doris's goddaughter Anyae' Elise (9) is a mentor to her little sister Savonne Noelle (5).

As you begin your day, make a decision to offer friendship, guidance, and encouragement to another person. You don't need special skills, just the ability to care and listen.

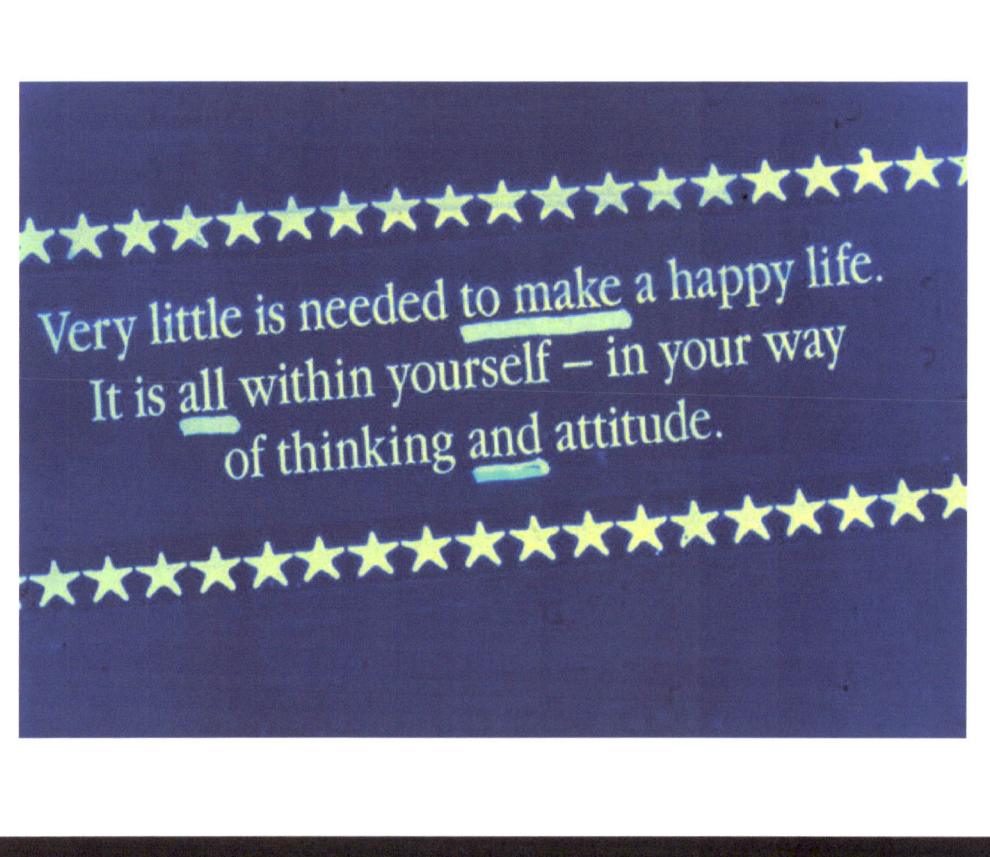

ATTITUDE IS EVERYTHING!

Friends with Attitude: Jordyn (9), Iman (9), Telia-Denise (9), and Eva-Leigh (11).

Friends brighten each others day. They see sunshine, not rain. When someone tries to rain on their parade, they focus on the positive. With a positive attitude, you can brighten someone else's day. Even cars run low on motor oil and we have to add a quart. If you think you're having a bad day, just add a quart of positive attitude and enjoy the rest of your day.

OVERCOME
Negative Thinking or Negative Mental Attitudes

When you feel some people don't like you and are always trying to rain on your parade, nothing will be gained by holding on to this negative thought. Choose the right attitude. Listen to YOURSELF as you talk to yourself about hopeful things. A positive attitude can make you feel like you have sunshine, even on a rainy day. Think positively!

Nothing can stop a person with the right attitude from achieving his or her goal; nothing on earth can help a person with the wrong attitude. Don't allow anyone to *ruin* your day by raining on your parade! When some less informed person has tried to ruin your day by giving you a hard time, don't react as he or she would. Don't mimic the bad attitudes of others. Overcome negativity by thinking positively! Just smile it off! Rise above it!

THE EVERETT FAMILY

The Everett family's closeness is a powerful way to boost their decision-making power. There is a special closeness that takes place when the family comes together to discuss life's challenges and the choices made yesterday.

The Everett Family

My "other daughter" Regina (center) believes family closeness is the key to staying connected with the girls in the family. Closeness and bonding among the girls helps to promote safe and healthy choices for the future. Back Row: Renee Williams (the student nanny), Natalie's daughter Kadence, and twin nieces Natalie and Nicole; with daughter Cariel; Chris (3) – not shown. Front row: daughters Lindsey, Layla, and Eve.

THE EVERETT FAMILY

The Everett family sets aside a specific time to reconnect and look for ways to make healthier life choices for the future. Today our world exists because of CHOICES.

The Everett Family

My "other son" Rey (center) believes it is important for all of his children, nieces, and cousins to stay connected by coming back home for family closeness. Rey is also dedicated to spending quality time with his sons to encourage healthy choices. Back row: Freddie. Front row: Josiah, Rey (Julius Sr.), and Julius Jr.

THE McNEIL FAMILY

My niece Gailyn and her husband Craig are committed to helping their two daughters Anyae' and Savonne grow up in a happy and stable environment, with the freedom and support to make right choices in life.

The McNeil Family

**My "niece" Gailyn and husband Craig value their children and put forth every effort to ensure their well-being. It is important for their two girls to know that their parents will stay connected and involved in their lives to help make right choices. Back row: Craig and Gailyn.
Front row: Savonne Noelle (5) and Anyae' Elise (9).**

THE BAKER FAMILY

My friends Jeffrey and his wife Sue enjoy spending quality time with their three daughters Christina, Danielle, and Adriana. They vacation together and enjoy hearing about their goals and interests. The relationship they have with their daughters allows them to take a personal interest in the best choices for their college education and friends.

**Parents Sue and Jeffrey (center).
Daughters Danielle (left), Christina, and Adriana.**

THE GILLES FAMILY

Our niece Becky and her husband Dennis encourage their two sons, Sam and Reece, to stay connected with family and to live with positive values which include: right choices, respect and courtesy, even when playing sports. Family is important to the Gilles Family.

The Gilles Family

Dennis, niece Rebecca (Becky), and sons Sam and Reece

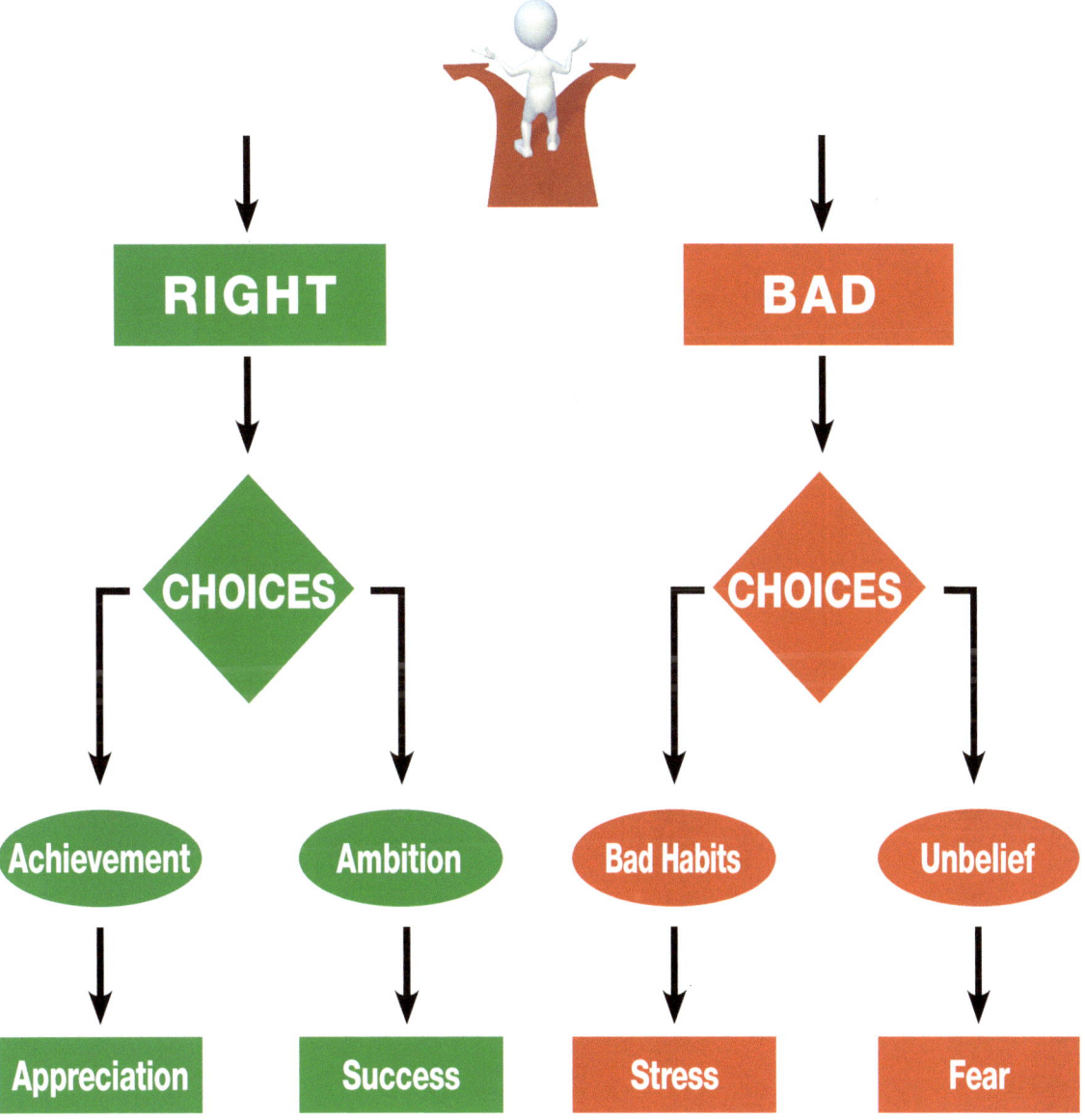

ATTITUDE: The WINNER'S Edge! • 105

ATTITUDE STORY
Unknown Origin

There once was a woman who woke up one morning, looked in the mirror, and noticed she had only three hairs on her head. "Well," she said, "I think I'll braid my hair today." So she did ,and she had a wonderful day.

The next day she woke up, looked in the mirror, and saw that she had only two hairs on her head. "Hmmm..," she said, "I think I'll part my hair down the middle today." So she did, and she had a grand day.

The next day she woke up, looked in the mirror and noticed that she had only one hair on her head. "Well," she said, "Today I'm going to wear my hair in a ponytail." So she did, and she had a fun, fun day.

The next day she woke up, looked in the mirror, and noticed that there wasn't a single hair on her head. "YAY!" she exclaimed. "I don't have to fix my hair today!"

———

Attitude is everything. There is very little difference in people, but that little difference makes a big difference. The little difference is attitude. The big difference is whether it is positive <u>or negative</u>.

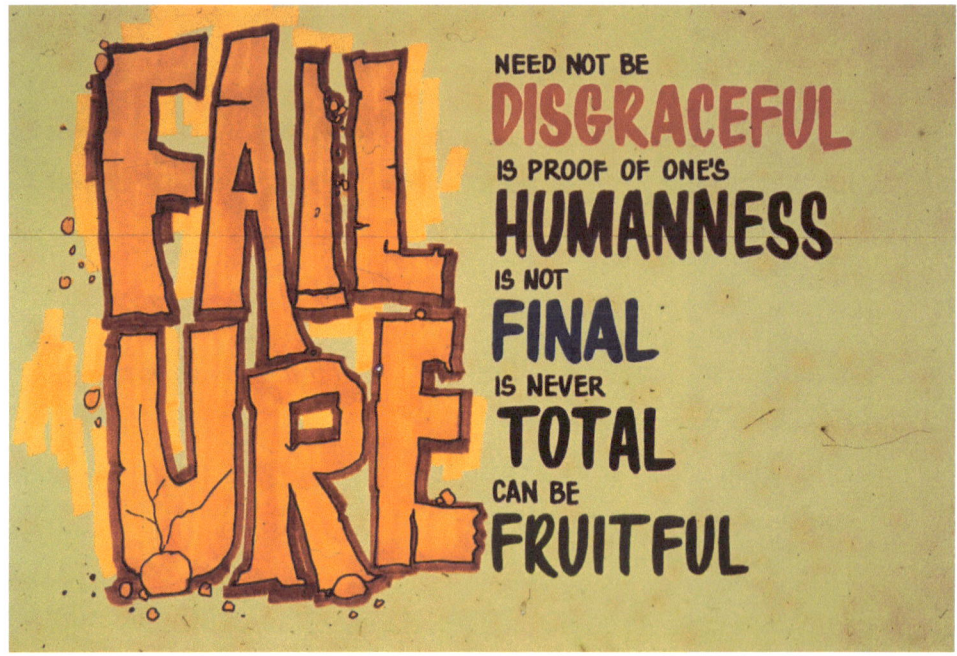

A Mistake Is Not a Failure

Every Accomplishment—Great or Small—Starts With The Same Decision:

"I'LL TRY."

FEAR of failure does influence our attitude. If you have the fear of failure, honestly face the possibility that your attitude may be the cause. Take responsibility. Be honest. If you are afraid to face up honestly about your attitude in life, you may be afraid to see YOU as you really are. KNOW who you really are. Accept yourself! Believe in yourself! It is the only way to get rid of fear.

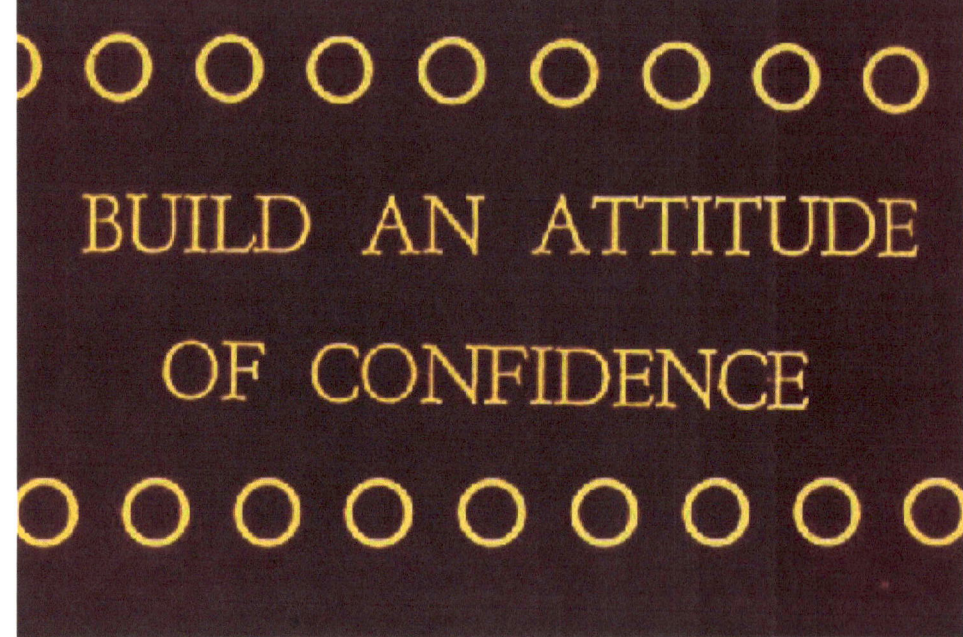

Feed your attitude with good thoughts daily. Learn to develop good attitudes by dwelling on things that are good. If you dwell on negative thoughts, your attitude will reflect negative thoughts. Your attitude in life will determine your success in life. The key is to act as the person you want to become. Ask yourself the following questions:

- Do I always do my best?
- Am I friendly and cooperative?
- Do I attend to details?
- Am I optimistic?
- Do I do more than my share?
- Am I well-mannered?
- Do I follow through?
- Am I believable?

You're not finished when you're defeated... you're finished when you quit.

Abraham Lincoln rose from humble beginnings. He had less than a year of formal education prior to running for political office. Before becoming President of the United States, Abraham Lincoln endured a steady stream of failure and defeat. He was born into poverty. He could have quit, but he didn't. He never gave up! Here is the list of "Failures of Abraham Lincoln"[8]:

Here is a common list of the failures of Abraham Lincoln (along with a few successes):

- 1831 - Lost his job
- 1832 - Defeated in run for Illinois State Legislature
- 1833 - Failed in business
- 1834 - Elected to Illinois State Legislature (**success**)
- 1835 - Sweetheart died
- 1836 - Had nervous breakdown
- 1838 - Defeated in run for Illinois House Speaker
- 1843 - Defeated in run for nomination for U.S. Congress
- 1846 - Elected to Congress (**success**)
- 1848 - Lost re-nomination
- 1849 - Rejected for land officer position
- 1854 - Defeated in run for U.S. Senate
- 1856 - Defeated in run for nomination for Vice President
- 1858 - Again defeated in run for U.S. Senate
- 1860 - Elected President (**success**)

EVERYTHING IS **WON** BY THOSE WHO **BELIEVE**

Abraham Lincoln's résumé looks like a pretty glum, making you wonder how he ever made it to the top. But when you really think of it, to run for office or high positions so many times, you have to have something on the ball and have more successes than meet the eye.

Abraham Lincoln is an excellent example of *the power of a new attitude*. He never quit trying and his positive attitude for success was key to his election as the 16th President of the United States.

Thomas Edison failed thousands of times while attempting to invent the light bulb. He is reported to have said that the attempts were not failures but opportunities to know how <u>not</u> to create a light bulb. Shortly thereafter, Edison invented the light bulb. A mistake is not a failure.

How to Develop the Critical Attitude for Success . . . The Winner's Edge

Always be positive. Think success, not failure. Nothing can stop the person with the right mental attitude from achieving his or her goal; nothing on earth can help the person with the wrong mental attitude. Say to yourself: "The problem is not the problem. The problem **is** my attitude **about** the problem."

Success or failure in life is determined more by our attitude than by our mental capacities. The most powerful force is what we say to ourselves. Build an attitude of confidence. Believe in yourself!

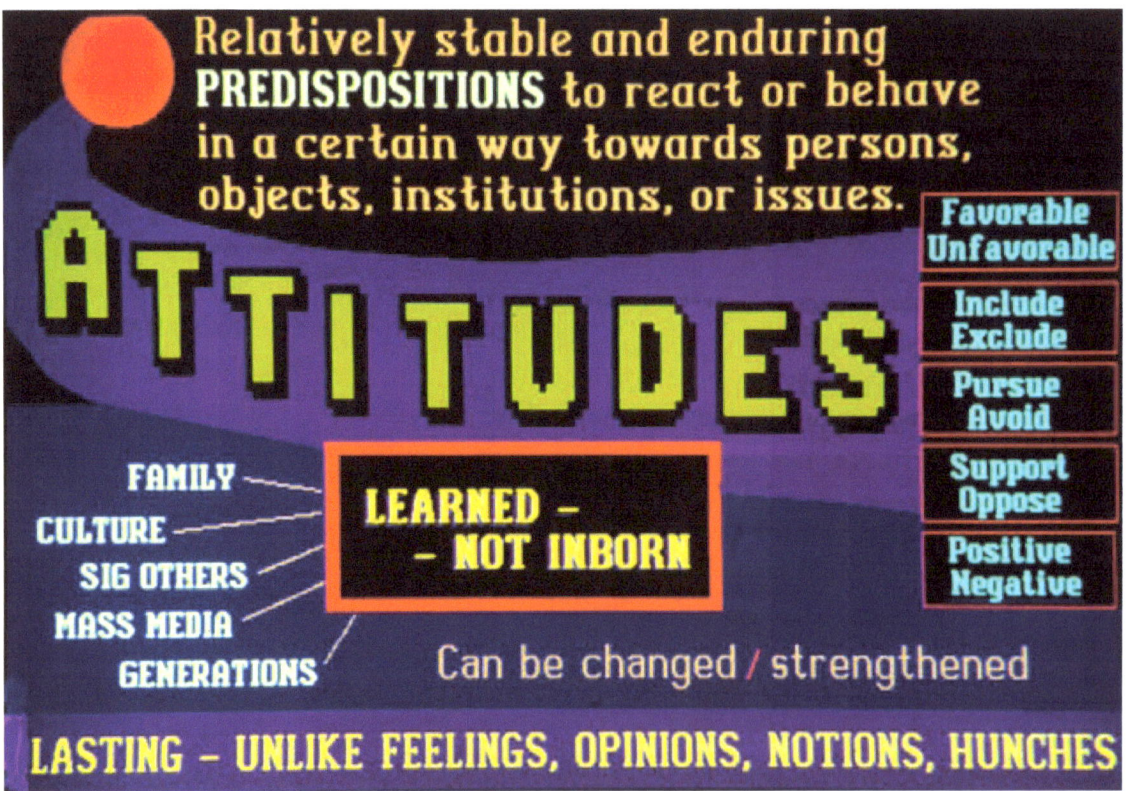

INSIDE STORY

If: A B C D E F G H I J K L M
    1 2 3 4 5 6 7 8 9 10 11 12 13

   N O P Q R S T U V W X Y Z
   14 15 16 17 18 19 20 21 22 23 24 25 26

Then: **H - A - R - D - W - O - R - K**
      8 + 1 + 18 + 4 + 23 + 15 + 18 + 11 = 98%

And **K - N - O - W - L - E - D - G - E**
    11 + 14 + 15 + 23 + 12 + 5 + 4 + 7 + 5 = 96%

But, **A - T - T - I - T - U - D - E**
     1 + 20 + 20 + 9 + 20 + 21 + 4 + 5 = **100%**

Therefore, one can conclude with mathematical certainty that Hard work and Knowledge will get you close, but it's your Attitude that will take you to the top …and Beyond!

ATTITUDE: The WINNER'S Edge!

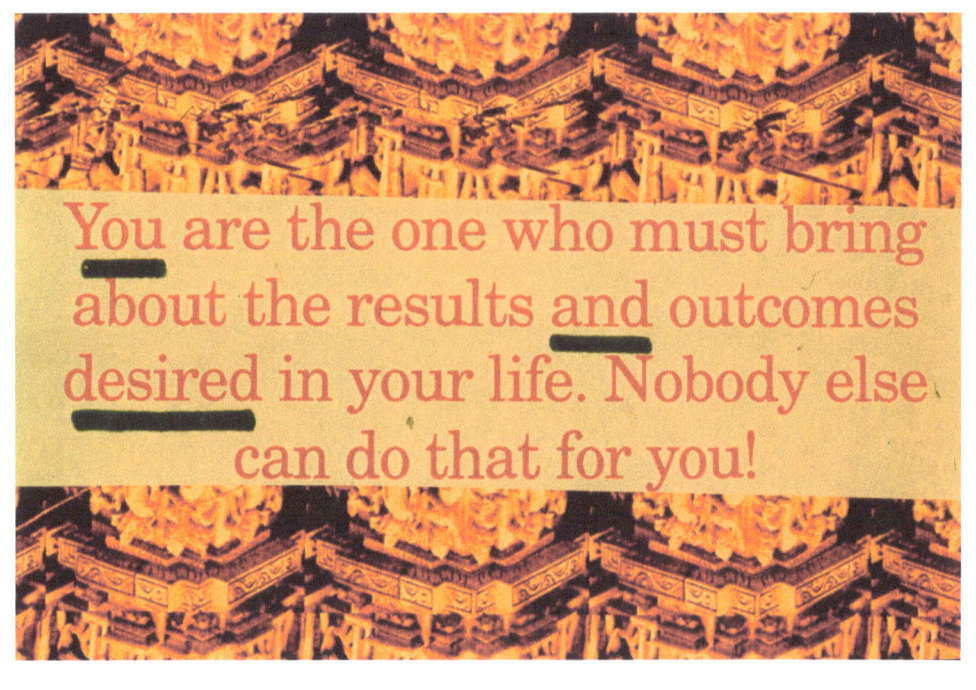

The Attitude Golden Rule

For the next 30 days treat everyone with whom you come in contact as the most important person on EARTH

30-DAY ATTITUDE GOLDEN RULE

For the next thirty (30) days, treat everyone the way he or she wishes to be treated. Choose to have a positive attitude and make a difference in the world. Every day, wake-up and tell yourself **"My attitude matters!"** My positive attitude is the secret to my success today.

ATTITUDE
ATTITUDE

At beginning of task, will affect outcome MORE than anything else.

Toward life (others) DETERMINES life's (other's) attitude toward us.

Radiate WELL BEING and confidence that you KNOW where you are going.

Look for the BEST in all new ideas & look for GOOD ideas everywhere

MAKE others feel needed, important, & appreciated, & they'll return same.

Act "AS IF" you are the person you want to become.

Most people don't think that their attitudes matter. They wake up and react to whatever happens to them. Don't react. Your attitude is something that can be controlled. Our attitude determines who is rider and who is horse. You have a choice. You either ride life or it rides you. The secret to the success in your life is a positive attitude!

Attitude! Attitude! Attitude! You have the power to choose your *attitude.* Remove the word "can't" from your vocabulary. The moment you say to yourself, "I can't", "you won't". Remember— positive things happen to *positive people!*

The Changing of Your Attitude

Attitudes can be infectious. Most people want to feel recognized, Appreciated, and needed. Most people want to feel that they count. When they feel these things, they will give their love and respect, and they will buy whatever products you sell. For the next thirty days, treat others the way they want to be treated, and they will return the favor.

Remember: Good Attitude = Good Results!

AN INSPIRATIONAL MEMOIR

By Nicole Colosimo

This memoir was written based on a high school assignment. Students were permitted to choose any person of any race or background who had made a positive difference in their life. The only condition was that the person could not be a relative. This young white female student chose the author of this book and asked permission to interview her. This paper was written during the interview.

As an African-American growing up in Alabama, nothing came easy for Doris Gothard. She started working as a child in the cotton fields all day. Now she is a highly respected person in the city of Detroit.

Doris, her two sisters, and brother grew up on a farm. They had many chores to do, but maybe harder than chores was Doris's job. Early in the morning a truck would drive by honking its horn, and all the children in the area would get on it to go to the cotton field. They would get up, dress in long pants and shirts, and pick cotton all day. They each had a sack with a tar bottom so that it could be dragged, but Doris carried the sack on her back even though it would sometimes be holding one hundred and fifty to two hundred pounds of cotton. Doris set a record of six hundred pounds a day. The school knew her family was poor and needed the money, so they sent the children's school work home. As tough as it was, Doris maintained straight A's åand A-'s and graduated as salutatorian.

In 1960, when Doris took her SAT, she scored so high, she was selected to go to President John F. Kennedy's White House Conference on Youth and Children. Before the school would let her go, they put Doris through classes to teach her how to stand, walk, eat, talk and dress. The experience was good for her because it gave her a chance to share experiences with people from other states.

Throughout school Doris wanted to be a doctor, but she knew it cost too much money, so she decided to become a school teacher instead. Doris went to Wright State University, and graduated with a degree in pure mathematics, with a minor in engineering. Doris taught math because of the degree and German because of her dog. When she was younger, she had a dog named Rommel Messerschmitt. It was a German dog. One day Rommel was stolen. He was Doris's best animal friend. She hasn't had another animal since because no one could take his place.

Doris has many stories to tell about growing up. One day when she and her sister were outside doing chores, Doris told her little sister that if she did her chores for her, she could have a tomato. Doris's sister loved tomatoes, so she said yes. Doris went and got a red pepper and told her sister to close her eyes and eat fast. She said that the tomato would be crunchy, but good. Her sister ate the pepper and started screaming. Their mom ran out and found out what happened. Doris can't remember a time that she got into more trouble except the time she took her mom's favorite high heels.

When Doris was around eleven, she wanted to wear high heel shoes more than anything, but her mom told her she was too young. Doris snuck into her mom's closet, and took her favorite red high heels. She went out in the backyard and started walking down a big hill. Doris fell and broke her arm. The day she got her cast off, her mom said

"From now on, you know to obey me. Don't wear my high heel shoes anymore." Doris wanted to know why she fell though, so she went into her mom's closet, took the same pair of red high heel shoes, and went out in the backyard. She started walking down the same big hill, fell, and broke the same arm again. Doris learned her lesson and never disobeyed her parents again.

Doris has won many awards, including the 4H achievement award, and the YMCA achievement award. Doris also won a national achievement award for the Future Homemakers of America. She was the first African-American to do so. In eleventh grade, she won the Miss Tan Alabama award. This beauty pageant was just like one of today's. For her special talent in the beauty contest, Doris gave a speech. Today she makes a lot of speeches because of her role on her job.

Doris enjoys working for her company because it provides opportunities and something different all the time. She gets to travel and meet new people, which is another thing she likes. Doris encourages employees to do volunteer activities. She goes into Detroit, paints houses, and takes food and clothes to the people who need it. She says that helping people is very rewarding and is glad that her company supports community outreach.

A major part of her community outreach is her role in DAPCEP, or Detroit Area Pre-College Engineering Program. Doris works with African-American, underprivileged inner-city kids from ninth to twelfth grade. She travels to schools and talks to students and helps them see they can be whatever they want to be. Most of the kids have a low self-esteem and don't think that they can be good at anything. Doris helps make them feel better about themselves. She feels that it takes a talent to understand that kids have needs, and she feels that she has that talent. Doris loves kids, she thinks that most kids are bright; that is why she does DAPCEP. In her speeches, Doris tells the kids two main things. One, the key to success is attitude. If you show someone a good attitude, they'll show you a good attitude back. Two, the reason most kids don't do well in school is because of peers. Peers, as she says, stands for Persons Encouraging Errors, Rudeness and Stupidity. She says that friends will not encourage you to do something bad, but your peers will. In all the times she has worked with young people, the thing she's most proud of is making a difference in at least one young person's life.

As one experience shows, she has made a difference in a lot of young people's lives. Last year a high school student called her and asked her if she would be the commencement speaker at their graduation. Doris agreed to do it. When she got there, there were cards, people, and police everywhere. She made her way to the school and found the principal. He said to her, "Doris, I'm so glad you made it,. I thought you would have to cancel also." Doris asked him what he meant, and he told her that Mayor Archer was supposed to be the speaker, but he couldn't make it, so they called her. When she got up to make her speech she said, "I know you're disappointed to see that I'm not Mayor Dennis Archer, but if you give me a chance, this will be the best fifteen minutes of every student's life." When she was done, the students gave her a standing ovation.

Last year, Doris and her husband moved into a new house. Doris designed it by herself. It took two years. The house is three floors of detail. Channel 4 did a special on her home, showing a mirrored wall that Doris also designed. Doris said "I think I planned it real well." One of Doris's hobbies is cooking. She makes the best cheesecake. In her house, Doris has two full-sized kitchens.

Another one of Doris's hobbies is fishing. She loves to fish. One time she was fishing in the St. Joseph River, and all morning she didn't get one bite. In the afternoon when she finally got one, it was so big she spent a half an hour reeling in and pulling. The line went slack and she thought she lost it. All the boats on the lake turned off their engines to calm down the lake and try to find the fish. Doris was upset that she lost her fish, and out from nowhere the fish came up and went under the boat. He was still on the line, so Doris started reeling in and pulling, and after another fifteen minutes, she finally got him. It was a Chinook Salmon that weighed thirty-nine and a half pounds, and it was thirty-eight inches long. To this day her fish still hangs over her fireplace.

Doris has a son LeWayne who is a singer. He just signed a record deal with Warner Brothers. Her husband, Don, is also very inspirational. He is an engineer and executive for General Motors and was on loan to NASA for the Apollo Space Program. He won the national Black Engineer of the Year award this year.

I think that I'm very lucky to have someone in my life like Doris. She is not only inspirational to me, but to most of the people she meets. She is a caring person and a great role model.

See teacher's comments and grade below.

WOW!
How did this remarkable woman become a part of your life? You are truly blessed to know her.

$$\frac{A}{A-}$$

The Stages of Your Life

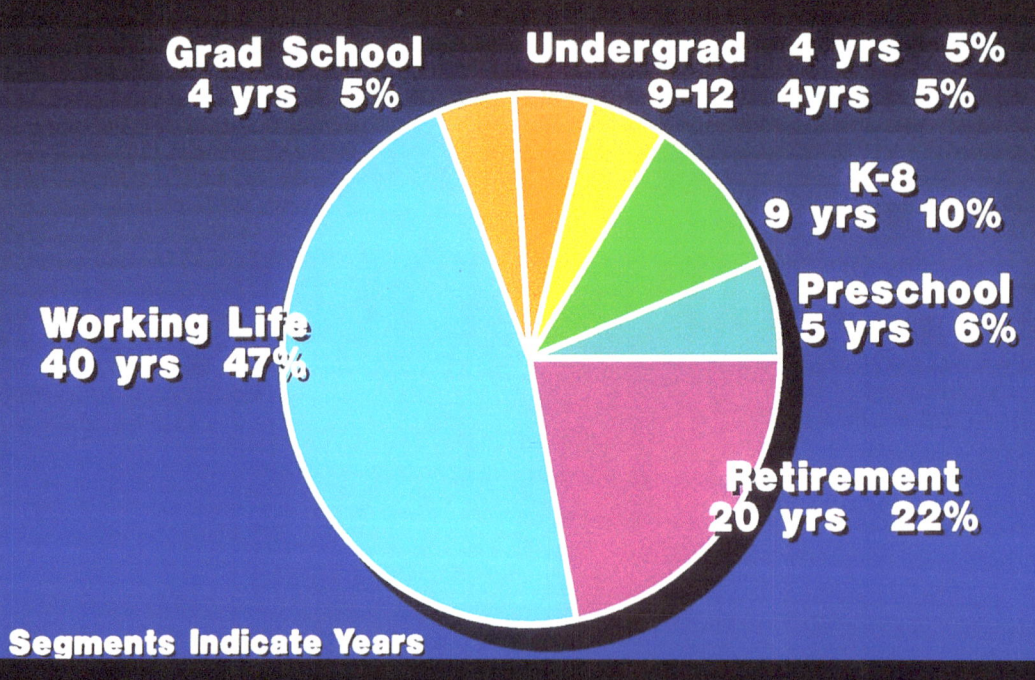

"THE STAGES OF LIFE"

Written By **Donald L. Gothard**
Retired GM Executive,
Washington, Michigan

Lou Holtz said it best when he said, "Ability is what you're capable of doing. Motivation determines what you do. Attitude determines how well you do it."[9]

Think about the stages of your life. Let's assume you have a life span of 86 years. You spend five years of your life at home before going to school. You spend nine years of your life in kindergarten through eighth grade. You'll then spend four years of your life in ninth grade to twelfth grade. If you graduate from high school and go on to a college or university, you may spend four years of your life preparing yourself for a career of some sort. If you move on to graduate school to get an advanced degree, you might spend another four years of your life finishing your preparations for a future career. You might even spend five years getting your undergraduate degree and five years in graduate school getting your advanced degree. This would add another two years to your schooling. However, for this example, let's just consider that your schooling will take up 26 years or 31% of your total life.

When you have finished with your schooling, then you will begin your working life stage. Let's assume you will work until you are

66 years old before you retire. This 40-year span takes up 47% of your life. When you retire you will have a life of 20 years left, or 22% of your total life span. All together you will have a period of 60 years, or 69% of your life, remaining after educating yourself for your work and retirement years. If you do not go on to college after high school, you will have to add another eight years to your working life. Consider the kind of life you'll have if you do not prepare yourself for a working life that you should want to enjoy. Consider what the 20 years in retirement will be like if you have not prepared yourself for retirement. If you only have Social Security to provide you with income in your retirement years, you'll be living at the poverty level. It will be even worse than that if Social Security is not available to you in the future.

In conclusion, your school years are the most important years in your life to prepare you for the majority years remaining in your life after school. What all individuals must ask themselves is, "What kind of life do I want to have for the majority years of my life?" A lot will depend on what your attitude on life during your preparation years in school will be. It's up to you to make the right decisions throughout your lifetime. This book is an attempt to provide the guidelines needed to change your attitude and develop an attitude for success.

A Final Glimpse of Our Attitude

Dear Winners,

We must take ownership of our attitude – an idea inspired by the life and work of Dr. G. Herbert "Herb" True. The ways in which we live and respond are the keys to developing a positive attitude. I would consider myself to have failed had it not been for the mentoring I received from my family about my attitude and my actions. Everything they said and did was centered on helping me to be the best I could be in life. My attitude reflects tremendous love and respect to my family and friends. Attitude is everything.

My strong belief in attitudes which demonstrate obedience, cooperation, and endurance instills self-confidence when I experience unfairness, disappointment, or tragedy. Like most people, I have felt misunderstood and in need of someone to help me refocus on my goals. I want to share a "perspective on attitude" written by my husband Don, who gave me the inspiration for writing this book:

ATTITUDE

> The importance of attitude was certainly demonstrated when I worked with the General Motors team that designed, built, tested, and installed the guidance and navigation systems for the Apollo Spacecraft. The attitude of the design team was always positive, and there was never a thought that we would not get our astronauts to the moon before Russia. Failure was not an option.
>
> Also, within my 40 years working as a General Motors engineer and executive, I had the privilege to work

with a group of young, dedicated engineers and students for 5 years as the executive responsible for advanced vehicle engineering at the GM Truck Division. These engineers and students only had thoughts on being successful. We had the responsibility to design vehicles and systems that had never been seen before. We had to think 5 to 10 years into the future. We had to demonstrate them to our General Motors top management, at annual auto and truck shows, and to writers for the many truck magazines that the public read.

I was particularly proud of the students who worked for me during the summer months. They were given assignments that were vital to our mission and very difficult to perform. The older engineers were always amazed, and we all would say, "They didn't know what they couldn't do." All had the attitude for success, and they always found a way to accomplish their assignments within the time period that we gave them. Two that I have kept in touch with now have positions as President and Vice President of the companies in which they are employed. I don't know where the others are, but I'm sure they are successes somewhere. Attitude is the key to success."

– Donald L. Gothard
Retired General Motors Executive

ATTITUDE: The WINNER'S Edge will help you live the kind of life that everyone will want to be a part of. May you experience the joy of lifelong friendships to keep you on the right track, with someone who is an encourager to help you accomplish your mission, a supporter and helper in achieving your goals, a confidant and best friend – just like my sister Roxie.

With Deepest Affection,

Doris

The Power of Friendships

....The Winner's Edge!

The Power of Friendships

Doris's great nephew, Gerger (left) had the courage to take the microphone and prove he could be the emcee of the program. *That's attitude!*

Gervase II's (Gerger's) friend Liliana (right) had the courage to stand up and prove she could be a professional singer. *That's attitude!*

The Power of Laughter and Beauty

Doris's brother-in-law Pete (left) enjoys a laugh with Enrique, who told a joke with confidence. *That's attitude!*

Izairis (right) poses for a picture and shows off her style, grace, charm and beauty. *That's attitude!*

....The Winner's Edge!

THE END

END NOTES

1. Text copyright 1973 Herbert Sass from the book *The American Eagle* by Tom and Pat Leeson, reprinted with permission from Beyond Words Publishing, Hillsboro, Oregon.

2. *Merriam Webster Collegiate Dictionary (11th ed.).* Springfield, MA: Merriam Webster, Inc., 2003. p.80.

3. Graham, Jerry. "Birds of a Feather." *The Coaching Pair.* 2011. Web. 14 May 2011. <http://thecoachingpair.com/blog/birds-of-a-feather>.

4. "Thoughts on the Business of Life." *Forbes.com.* 2010. Web. 14 May 2011. <http://thoughts.forbes.com/thoughts/example-robert-half-if-birds-of>.

5. Van Oech, Roger. *A Whack on the Side of the Head.* New York: Warner Books, 2008. Print.

6. Galasso-Vigorito, Catherine. "A Great Attitude Paves the Way for Great Results." *The Macomb Daily.* 21 Jan. 2011. Web. 1 June 2011. <http://www.macombdaily.com/articles/2011/01/29/lifestyles/srv0000010662528.txt>.

7. McCay, James T. *The Management of Time.* New York: Prentice Hall, 1995. p. 165. Print.

8. Kurtus, Ron. "Failures of Abraham Lincoln." *School for Champions.* 11 January 2007. Web. 14 May 2011. <http://www.school-for-champions.com/history/lincoln_failures.htm>.

9. Holtz, Lou. *Quotations Book.* 2007. Web. 14 May 2011. <http://quotationsbook.com/quote/3467/#axzz1LXho4OLV>.

www.ingramcontent.com/pod-product-compliance
Lightning Source LLC
Chambersburg PA
CBHW041549220426
43666CB00002B/14